T0090776

FINDING
PEACE
THRU THE
STORMS
OF LIFE

Eva Ashe

authorHOUSE®

AuthorHouse™
1663 Liberty Drive
Bloomington, IN 47403
www.authorhouse.com
Phone: 833-262-8899

Published by AuthorHouse   03/24/2022

ISBN: 978-1-6655-5250-9 (sc)
ISBN: 978-1-6655-5262-2 (e)

Print information available on the last page.

Any people depicted in stock imagery provided by Getty Images are models, and such images are being used for illustrative purposes only. Certain stock imagery © Getty Images.

Scripture taken from the King James Version of the Bible.

This book is printed on acid-free paper.

Because of the dynamic nature of the Internet, any web addresses or links contained in this book may have changed since publication and may no longer be valid. The views expressed in this work are solely those of the author and do not necessarily reflect the views of the publisher, and the publisher hereby disclaims any responsibility for them.

Dedicated to God who never gave up on me but continued
to open doors of encouragement and inspiration.
Also, dedicated to my grandchildren,
Noah, Grayson, Adair and Ernie.

CONTENTS

DEVOTIONS

PRAYERS

DEVOTIONS

GOOD MORNING GOD

I walked out this morning to put some letters in the mailbox and I could hardly make myself go back inside. It had rained during the night and everything looked so fresh and clean. It was breath taking to see what God plans and creates just for our enjoyment.

The birds were chirping, bringing sweet music through the air. From the left was the sound of big birds, probably those big black crows I never liked very much, but somehow seemed different this morning. From the right was the sound of the sweet little birds I love so much. Even when I can't see them far up in the trees, I enjoy their music early in the morning and look forward to seeing them on the patio.

I stood on the front porch in awe of God's wonderful world. For a moment, I stood silent and thought about those who never experienced a moment like this, "Just God and me." I pray that they, too, will someday meet God in a very meaningful way. May God bless them.

I know today is going to be a good day.

A FORGIVING GOD

Jesus Christ is the only man or person who ever lived a perfect, sinless life on earth and he sacrificed his life so we could be forgiven of our sins and have eternal life.

Many times people will not join the church or make a personal confession because they feel they cannot live up to God's expectations. Others see the sins of some church members and they turn away from church. We do not go to church to observe the sins of others but to focus on God and have a relationship with him. He is a forgiving God, and he loves us in spite of our sins.

Who his own self bare our sins in his own body on the tree, that we, being dead to sins, should live unto righteousness: by whose stripes ye were healed. 1 Peter 2:24

A LESSON IN ART

A great piece of art touches the mind, heart and soul of the viewer. Art is all about composition, balance, and use of light in the painting. It stirs the viewer's emotions and makes one want to keep looking and never get tired viewing it. The rhythm and color manipulation contributes to a good piece of art. A painting should not be overworked but should leave something for the viewer's imagination.

With these thoughts in mind, I have written the following wedding vows.

A PERFECT PIECE OF ART

You and me, we make a perfect piece of art.
With harmony and unity,
We fit together, you and me.
You and me, we make a perfect piece of art.

You put a ring upon my finger
And love into my heart.
You said, "If God is on our side,
We'll never, ever part."

We'll climb the hills together.
We'll gaze upon the moon.
We'll pray to God our life will be
Like one big honeymoon.

When life gets dull and boring
We'll have a kid or two
And that will surely bring us joy
And contrast in life too.

You and me, we'll make a perfect piece of art.
With harmony and unity,
We'll fit together, you and me.
You and me, we'll make a perfect piece of art.

Lord, thank you for the people you have put in my
path to encourage me and give me inspiration.

A LITTLE TALK WITH GOD

Lots of things I don't understand,
Like why is life so short for some
Or why good people wait in fear,
Afraid to see my Jesus come.

I don't know why the storm clouds rage,
Or why you make the birds to sing.
I don't know why the rose has thorns,
Or why the flowers bloom in spring.

And that itsy, bitsy spider,
I don't like very much at all,
I wonder why you have made him
And why he's hanging from my wall.

When I look at the fluffy clouds
Or watch the angry, rolling sea,
I know my God is in control.
Could you have done this all for me?

But I don't need to know all this,
'Cause always with me you will be.
There's just one thing I'd like to know,
Please, dear Lord, why did you make me?

MOTHER'S LOVE

The greatest love on earth for another human being is probably the love of a mother. She will forgive her children when everyone else is against them. When we were born that everlasting love for us was instilled in her heart and when we are grown she loves us no less than she did when we were babies. We might have done some hurtful things, but that love shines through all the grief we caused her through the years.

There are times when a mother passes away and the ones left behind wish they could have said, "I love you," just one more time, but she knew her children loved her. There were times when things went wrong and they grieved because they hadn't asked for her forgiveness. She probably forgave them before they even thought about asking. A mother's love touches our lives in a very special way and it stays with us forever.

So, if you have a living mother, don't fail to say, "I love you." They are the sweetest words a mother could ever hear. Precious jewels and souvenirs don't compare with a little quality time one shares with a mother. A mother's love cannot be bought any more than the love of our Heavenly Father. He too, wants and deserves a little quiet time with His children. We never grow so old that we no longer have a need for more love and more wisdom.

A PLEA TO GOD AND
SOMEONE SPECIAL

Love me as I am and not that perfect person you would like me to be.

Don't expect me to always think like you. Even though I need your guidance, I also need to be free to think on my own and make my own decisions

Be patient with me for I am slow to get it right sometimes. My little brain needs time to sort things out and too much pressure confuses me.

Help me to be strong and give me the courage to face the difficult times of life.

Help me to love without expecting something in return.

Help me to be joyful and pleasant in all things I face in life.

Catch me if I fall along the wayside of righteousness. There is so much corruption in the world today, I could easily lose my way and I need to know you are standing by my side when I call on you.

Just let me always feel your touch and I will be the best that I can be.

For your love, your grace and your mercy, I will forever be grateful.

A SONG IN MY HEART

We all have our ups and downs in life. On the good days a little song from the heart can lift the spirit even higher. During the bad times you may have to dig deep down inside the heart to find a song, but you can do it. You don't have to be able to sing or even carry a tune, just find a song that has some meaning to you. Let it roll over and over in your mind even if you only know one line. You might find yourself singing them out loud and lifting them up to God. Sometimes it's hard to find the words you want to say to God, but somehow a few words from a song can say it all.

The other day I had something heavy on my mind and it was really stressing me out. I suddenly came out with the words, "Fill my cup, Lord. I lift it up, Lord." I went around the house singing the one line and could not think of any more of the song. I felt like I was singing to my Lord. I suddenly realized, my stress was gone but I had to know what the rest of the song was about. I could not find it in my hymnal so I went to the computer and found it. When I read the words, I felt like it was written just for me on that particular day. I know God must have planted that song in my heart.

Songs can be like prayers. The words can say exactly what you wanted to say to the Lord but somehow couldn't find them without a little help.

ANTELOPES

I remember reading an interesting article about African Antelopes. According to the writer, they are amazing creatures that can jump over a ten foot fence and cover a distance of thirty –three feet. Yet, they can be kept in a zoo inside an enclosure with a simple three foot wall because they cannot see where their feet will land on the other side of the wall.

Most of us are capable of taking great leaps of faith, but will not do so because we cannot see what the future holds on the other side of the wall. This is when we have to let faith take over. There are many, many decisions in life we have to make based on faith. Prayer is having faith that God will hear our request and fill our needs.

Yesterday is gone, today is all we have. Nobody knows what tomorrow holds, so we make plans for tomorrow, not knowing what it holds, but having faith that our future will be according to God's will.

ARE YOU HAPPY WITH YOURSELF

You can never grow as a person until you learn to accept who you are and work to correct your flaws.

Do not be envious of others. They may not be as perfect as you think.

Celebrate the simple pleasures in life. Don't wait for a birthday or holiday to celebrate. Find joy in the little things life has to offer. Sometimes we have to make the best of what life hands us.

Learn to be confident. Appreciate the things that make you unique. Everyone is insecure about something. Recognize your mistakes, then let them go, only then can you focus on the future. Don't try to blame someone else for your unhappiness. You will never be happy as long as you are trying to place the blame for your unhappiness on someone else.

If you are a healthy person, be thankful. There are people whose lives revolve around their problems. Do what you can to help those less fortunate than you. Add a little laughter to your life. Laughter is contagious, so be around people who love to laugh.

Are you happy with your body? Exercising and eating healthy can help both mind and body. Planning a good balance between fruits and vegetables, proteins and carbs can make you feel much healthier and more in tune with your body.

Your deepest, most lasting happiness will come from faith in God and developing God-like attributes such as goodness, love, justice and mercy. We need to overcome the desires of the human body and follow the teachings of Jesus Christ. Happiness is a part of that enter peace and joy that comes from God. It requires nothing of others. It's just a gift God gives when you are truly connected with Him and His inconceivable joy.

BLESSINGS FROM HEAVEN

For some unknown reason, one of the songs from the Oldies, "Pennies from Heaven," keeps boggling my mind. It begins like this: "Every time it rains, it rains pennies from Heaven. Don't you know each cloud contains pennies from Heaven?" Then it goes on to say, "Be sure your umbrella is upside down." That is so you can catch those pennies from Heaven.

Let's look at this from a different point of view. Let's try changing this to, "Blessings from Heaven." All good things come from God. In the midst of crisis, He gives us hope. He promises us contentment in every situation. He controls the storms of life. God gives us peace abundantly and we should accept it thankfully. He loves us with an unconditional love and when we start to feel afraid, He is our shield.

God's presence accompanies us and will continue to accompany us all the days of our life. Using His name frequently would be a great reminder of His daily presence in our life.

There is no need for us to turn our umbrella upside down to catch all these blessings God has in store for us. With that unconditional love He has for us along with His grace and mercy He so freely gives, He will shower us with blessings for all our needs.

When we have lost our way or feel the need to call on Jesus, we simply need to say, "Help me, Jesus, I cannot find my way."

CHANGE

Sometimes change comes really hard, but there are times that change is necessary. We often find change especially difficult to deal with when its existence has been with us for a lifetime. Our personal life changes and we have to adjust.

A business has to make changes when it no longer fulfills its purpose. We often see store fronts change in order to attract more customers. Even if the store carries the right goods to sell, something has to change to attract people so they will enter the door.

There are many changes from one generation to another. Popular music from yesterday is quite different than the popular music today. Church services, and its music, have changed from traditional to contemporary. Sometimes we have to change with the times.

If we are not happy with our life or the circumstances around us, we need to make changes. Life is full of challenges. Maybe we should all take a good look at ourselves to see if there are some changes we need to make.

May God shower his blessings upon his children. He loves each and every one of us.

CYBERSPACE

I guess you could say I am a moderate user of the computer. It would be very hard to live in today's world without the use of a computer.

Knowing so little about cyberspace, I decided I would look up its definition. I found that there are 28 different definitions for the term cyberspace. One of the definitions was, "The national environment in which communication over computer networks occurs." There is no fully agreed official definition yet.

The internet is defined as a large group of computers that are connected together to be used to send information around the world.

The internet was created in the United States by the U S Department of Defense, Advance Research Projects Agency. It was first connected in October, 1969. The World Wide Web was created at CERN in Switzerland in 1989 by a British man named Tim Barners-Lee. To name just a few uses, the internet is used to send electronic mail, on line chats and E-mail.

The most used service on the internet is the World Wide Web. The second major use of the internet is to send and receive e-mails.

If man can create something as complicated as Cyberspace, why would anyone question the fact that God created the Heaven and the earth and all that is in it? If man can create something that can send messages all over the world in seconds, why would one question God being in all places at all times. He never tells us to wait 'cause he's too busy.

Why would anyone doubt that God hears our prayers? He has plans for our life but it is up to us to follow through with his plans. Sometimes we are too busy making our own plans to hear what God has in store for us.

DEATH AND GRIEF

In a quiet moment I was thinking about my neighbors and friends who have lost their spouse and the process one goes through when a spouse passes away.

Friends, family and loved ones gather around, offering comfort and respect while the one left behind puts on their best front. They go through a few days almost in denial that their loved one has been taken away.

Then the time comes when everyone leaves and later discontinues their daily calls and visits. Suddenly there comes the realization that, "It's just me and the Lord. We have to take responsibility for everything."

During times like this, loneliness can take over if you don't have God in your life. It is very important that friends stay in touch, lend a helping hand, and give encouragement. Don't just tell a grieving person they need to get out and be with friends. Instead, pick them up and be with them as they rejoin their outside friends. It is very hard to go out and face the world when you feel that your world has been destroyed. Everyone grieves differently. Some like to be alone for a few days. We have to respect that, while others need people and a lot of support. Those who are determined to be strong may try to hide their grief and think showing emotions can be a sign of weakness. But that doesn't make the pain any less. Then there are those who have to show their emotions as a way of dealing with the grief. I have a friend who has some concern that she never cried after her husband passed away. I have another friend who doesn't understand why she gets emotional and teary eyed so often.

God painted us all with a different brush and different strokes but there is one thing that will always remain the same. Learning to lean on Jesus is the best way to warm one's heart and rest one's mind while going through the uncertain times of life.

Death is a part of life on earth. As sure as we are born, we will also die on this earth. But, if we believe and trust in Jesus Christ, God will redeem our soul from the grave and give us eternal life.

DISCOVERING LOVE

There are many different kinds of love and we express them in different ways. We love our neighbor but we have a much stronger feeling for our mother. We love our friends but there may be one that is very special, one who is more trustworthy and will stand by our side through all our needs.

Let's look back at our preteen and teenage years. We thought we were falling in love every time one of our classmates flirted with us. That was probably the time of life when we were trying to learn what love is.

Do you remember your first real love, the one that will always hold a place in your heart? Even though you chose not to share the rest of your life with that person, there was something very special about the relationship. I recall reading an article long, long years ago that said, "even though you love a person, it doesn't mean that person is right for you."

Then one day you meet that "special" person and you vow to honor and love that person for the rest of your life. At that time you think it must be the happiest day of your entire life and no love could be greater. Earthly love can bring lots of joy but can also bring heartaches.

Love is hard to explain and it is not always easy to love someone. Love can mean different things to different people and under different circumstances.

Think back to the birth of your first child. Two people fell in love and with the help of God they made this beautiful little babe. When that little baby was placed in your arms, you thought it was the greatest love of all, the greatest miracle there could ever be.

Each kind of love is a little different than the other. But, there is one love that is greater than any of these. I'm not good at explaining this because I don't fully understand how this love can be so great. I have learned through life experiences, faith in God, and trusting in His word.

The amazing, unconditional love of God is the greatest love of all. He will forgive and love us regardless of all the sinful things we have done in our lifetime. He loves us so much that He gave His only begotten Son as a sacrifice for our sins, and whosoever believes in Him shall not perish but have eternal life. He promised He would prepare a place for us like no eye has ever seen. And, I have the faith to believe Him, even though I don't fully understand. God's awesome love is more than the human mind can ever understand or comprehend.

Thank you, Lord, for loving us. And thank you for your Son, Jesus Christ.

EASTER

Easter celebrates Jesus Christ's resurrection from the dead. Easter does not fall on the same date every year as most holidays. Christian Churches in the West celebrate Easter on the first Sunday following the full moon after the vernal equinox on March 21. Therefore, Easter is always observed anywhere between March 22 and April 25. I checked several definitions of vernal-equinox and some I did not understand. This was the simplest definition I could find. Taken from the Collins English Dictionary; vernal-equinox is the time at which the sun crosses the plane of the equator towards the relevant hemisphere making day and night of equal length.

Orthodox Christians use the Julian Calendar to calculate when Easter will occur and typically celebrate the holiday a week or two after the western churches, which follows the Gregorian Calendar.

Now that we understand how we arrive at the date of celebration, let's think about the resurrection that took place on the third day after Jesus was buried.

It is the power of our heavenly Father that raised Jesus Christ from the dead. Christ died for our sins and he was raised for our justification.

Romans 10:9 tells us, "if you confess with your mouth, 'Jesus is Lord' and believe in your heart that God raised him from the dead, you will be saved." Therefore, you cannot be a Christian unless you believe in the resurrection of Jesus Christ.

EMPTY PROMISES

As each New Year rolls in, many of us will make empty promises to ourselves. Maybe we can work on that a little and find it's worth our time to give it a try.

But, for now let's make a promise to God that we will pray daily. Each year brings greater challenges and obstacles in our life. Pray that God will give us courage, hope and faith to overcome all the hurdles we face in the future. Let's pray that love, peace and the joy of knowing God will find a permanent place in our heart. There's always something going on in our life that we can inprove.

FORGIVENESS

Some of the hardest tasks on earth are spiritual ones. It is not easy to return hate with love. It is not easy to admit you were wrong. It is hard to forgive without an apology from the one who hurt you. Forgiving is a difficult but necessary thing to do when you have been hurt, cheated, or betrayed.

Forgiveness is to release and let go of a past hurt, resentment, or negative feelings toward yourself and others. Forgiveness releases you from the past and allows you to be in the present.

The person who wronged you may not deserve to be forgiven for the heartache and grief they caused you, but your mind, body, and soul deserve to be free. Likewise, if you wronged yourself or someone else, self-forgiveness is just as important.

Holding on to a grudge or remaining a victim of someone else's bad behavior can cause stress, high blood pressure, and tightening of the muscles.

Learning to forgive makes us happier, healthier, and deepens our relationship with God. Pray for God to help you forgive when someone hurts you. Also, pray for the person who mistreated you. Prayer is one of the best gifts one can give or receive. It cost nothing but has lots of rewards.

Those heartless people who nailed Jesus to the cross and watched him die in great pain, never apologized to Him. In spite of their disrespectful behavior, Jesus prayed: "Father, forgive them; for they know not what they do." (Luke 23:34)

GOD'S AMAZING GRACE

In my heart I know what God's grace is but I keep searching for a definition that satisfies my desire to learn more about God's grace. So, I've been doing a little research just for my own satisfaction.

One of our most beautiful hymns is "Amazing Grace." The words are so well written and there are other hymns about grace also.

2 Peter 3:18 tells us to grow in the grace and knowledge of our Lord and Savior, Jesus Christ.

Hebrew 4:16 tells us to approach the throne of grace with confidence, so that we may receive mercy and find grace to help us in our time of need.

Ephesians 2:8 tells us it is by grace we have been saved. Anything good we experience is a result of God's grace.

Grace began in the Garden of Eden when Adam and Eve disobeyed God and ate from the tree of knowledge. God made garments of skin to cover them.

Grace is God's voluntary and loving favor given to those he saves. Without God's grace, no person can be saved. The only way to receive this loving favor is through faith in Jesus Christ.

Grace and mercy are not the same. Mercy is the deliverance from judgment or withholding a punishment we deserve. God's grace is a favor or a blessing we don't deserve but God gives it just the same.

And that is God's amazing grace!

GODLY THOUGHTS FOR THE NEW YEAR

Lord, we are so thankful that you helped us through another year. Now, we look forward to new adventures, new experiences, new wisdom and insight.

We are so blessed to live in America, the land of the free and home of the brave.

Lord, give us a loving heart and a joyous spirit. May the light from Your Glory shine upon each of us.

As we enter the New Year, may we leave the past where it belongs and move into the future with open hearts and minds to receive whatever God has in store for us. Let us not be so much in our own little world that we cannot see beyond ourselves.

Our God is an awesome God. May we give honor and praise to Him throughout the New Year.

HAPPY NEW YEAR

HAPPY FATHERS DAY

Everyone needs a father, not for just the early years of life, but a father is needed from the cradle to the grave. We need an earthly father and a Heavenly Father.

A father can, and should, love a child equally as much as a mother. A father can, sometimes, discipline a child with just the tone of his voice and it's not necessary to use harsh words. Remember the days when mothers would say, "If you don't behave I'm going to tell your Daddy." That's when you knew it was time to settle down and do what was right.

I wish the fathers of today would stop and realize how much they are needed in the life of a child. The father plays a very important role in a child's life. Many children are without a father in the home. A lot of kids go astray when they are not living under the guidance of a father. It is difficult for a mother to play the role of both father and mother. God created man and woman with different characteristics. They are both needed to conceive a child and both needed to raise a child.

Fathers, don't just love your children now and then. Let them know your love for them is a love without ending. Remember, it's ok for a father to say, "I love you." They are probably the most precious words you could ever say to your child.

HAPPY NEW YEAR

Maybe everything didn't go as we would
have liked in the past year. Maybe we, or
a family member, had a health problem.
Or, could it have been a marriage break-up?
No matter what the problem was, we still
have a lot of things for which we can be
thankful.

We can begin life anew any time we choose
and January seems to be a perfect time to
make changes. Everything has a beginning.
Resolutions are easy to make but are not
always easy to keep.

Let's try to be a cheerful person in spite of
the problems we encounter. Everyone loves
a cheerful person but no one likes to be
around a grump who complains about everything

We need to get rid of that ego. It can get in
the way of success. Get rid of the need to be right
and in control at all times. Getting control of
one's own life does not mean we need to control
others.

Let's set our goals for the New Year and
increase our self-confidence to achieve
those goals.

HAPPY NEW YEAR

HEAVEN CAME DOWN

When I was in elementary school, my close friends were planning to join the church. Being one of the group, I wanted to join also. I talked with my Mom about it and she thought I was too young and didn't understand what it meant. When I look back, I think she might have been right.

In my younger days I always felt a love for the Lord, in my own special way, and I read the Bible in bits and pieces. I didn't learn a lot but I just knew there was a God who loved me and I loved him. My family was not regular church goers but my Mom frequently made reference to the Lord.

After I grew up and was on my own, I was a regular attendant. Every Sunday as I listened to the sermon there was this yearning inside me to know and understand more about Jesus. There was this need to be closer to Jesus but I always waited until the next Sunday to make a public confession. Finally, when I could wait no longer, I walked down the aisle of my little country church and gave my heart and soul to Jesus Christ. I was in my early twenties when I finally took this step in my spiritual life. Walking down that aisle when I was younger would have been easier but I'm sure it would not have been as meaningful.

Yes, I finally did it! I walked down that aisle and gave my heart and soul to Jesus Christ. I have no words to adequately describe the relief and joy that filled the emptiness I previously experienced. It is best described by sharing the words of a favorite song, "Heaven Came Down."

Continue-----------

HEAVEN CAME DOWN

O what a wonderful, wonderful day
Day I will never forget;
After I'd wandered in darkness away,
Jesus my Savior I met.
O what a tender, compassionate friend
He met the need of my heart;
Shadows dispelling,
With joy I am telling,
He made all the darkness depart!

Heaven came down
And glory filled my soul,
When at the cross
The Savior made me whole;
My sins were washed away
And my night was turned to day
Heaven came down
And glory filled my soul.

Words and music by: John W. Peterson, 1921

INDEPENDENCE DAY

On July 4, 1776, the thirteen colonies claimed their independence from England. This eventually led to the formation of the United States. Today, the original copy of the Declaration is housed in the National Archives in Washington, D. C.

July 4 has been designated a national holiday to commemorate the day the United States laid down its claims to be a free and independent nation.

It is evident that all men are created equal and are endowed by their creator with certain rights. Among these are life, liberty, and pursuit of happiness. Yes, we are free to be happy, free to worship God as we wish, free to love and free to live our lives as we see fit. We refer to all these things as being free. But, freedom isn't free. Many lives have been sacrificed through the years so we can continue to be free. Mothers and Fathers have lost their sons and daughters to keep us free. At times I feel our freedom is slowly slipping away from us. There's always someone trying to take God out of public places, demanding Him to be taken off of His money and would like to take Him out of our country and out of our hearts. If we don't stand up for our faith, one day we might find that the Jesus we love so much has been swept right under the rug.

While enjoying the BBQ, the fellowship, and fun on the 4th of July, let's step back, take stock, appreciate the freedom we have, and give God all the Glory.

May God heal our country and save us as a Christian nation.

LEARN TO LET GO

There comes a time in life when we have to let go. We hold on to many things that have great meaning to us and things that bring back memories of days gone by. But, for most of us a time comes when we have to clean house and move on to the next or final stage of life. If we could condition our minds to accept that which we have no control over, we could make life easier and more enjoyable.

My suggestion to you is, when you have to leave your home, make up your mind before you go that you will be happy in your new residence. Take the necessary things and leave the rest behind. Let the kids get rid of the excess. They can get rid of things much easier than we can, and it will save a few tear drops along the way.

Remember, joy comes from within and everything is beautiful in its own way. After all, when you leave this world, the only thing you can take with you is your relationship with God, and you will have no desire to come back to this old world.

LONELINESS

Are you lonely? Some people are lonely even with people around them. If you are lonely, it is of your own choosing. All you have to do is take a look around you and you will know God is present.

Are you feeling depressed? Sit on the patio and look for things that indicate God's presence. Watch the birds and you will see that each one is different. Who could have done this other than God? Listen to them sing or communicate with one another. Look at the trees, notice the shape of the leaves and how they are attached to the limb. Look at the flowers, smell the fragrance and admire their beauty. This is all a part of God's creation. Do something to lift up someone else. Just a mere telephone call can sometimes mean the world to another person. And, you'll be glad you called.

Get the idea? God is so very close and you only need to invite him in. Enjoy God's wonderful creation. He made it for you!

And, behold, I am with thee, and will keep thee in all places whither thou goest, and will bring thee again into this land: for I will not leave thee, until I have done that which I have spoken to thee of.

Genesis 28:15

MAKE TODAY A GOOD DAY

So, yesterday was not a very good day!!!

That's the way life goes. God never promised life to be a bed of roses. If you don't create problems in your own pathway, someone will do it for you. Say, "Good Morning" to God and ask him to lead the way.

Make peace with yesterday so it don't screw up today. When your burdens are too much to bare, call a friend. When she gets through whining about her problems, you may feel better about yours. Visit a sick friend or homebound person, when you leave you are likely to say, "I'm so glad I visited her today, she really needed someone."

When you see a sad face, say a kind word. It might lighten the burden they are carrying. Always remember, when you brighten someone else's day, you also brighten your own.

MAKING TIME FOR GOD

We live in a world that has so many distractions it's hard to stay focused on God. Our strength comes from God, so it's important that we keep God close to our heart. In today's world, if we can plow through life's daily problems, fears and disappointments and still find time to talk with God, consider it a victory. We also need to find some quiet time so we can listen to God's plan and directions for our day.

Each day of our life is a glorious gift from God. Live it to the fullest but always have God in it. Take pleasure in leaning on God, instead of people. They can cause you to lose sight of God. Don't give people power over you. Always be yourself, the person God intended you to be.

Sometimes we have to stop everything momentarily and have a little talk with God. Any communication with him makes him happy. If you feel tempted, stressed or overcome with problems, talk it over with God. He understands better than anyone.

Talk with God just like you would talk with a friend. He is the greatest friend you will ever have. His love is unconditional and he will love you today, tomorrow and forever.

MORE THAN ONE CAN HANDLE

During a time of grief and sorrow, we try to comfort the ones who have been affected by death, sickness, disaster and such. We have often heard someone say, "God will not put more on you than you can handle." That is a common belief but is it really true? Is that what the Bible says? What the Bible does say is, "God is faithful; he will not let you be tempted beyond what you can bear." God will provide a way out so you can stand up under any temptation.

We were never promised an easy life on this earth but God loves us and no matter what difficulties we face, he will go through the tough times with us.

We need to understand that God is God as he presents himself through the Holy Scriptures. We should never lead one to believe life will be easy and all problems will be solved once a person becomes a Christian.

So long as the churches exist and the faithful gather to pray and worship, no one has to bear their burdens alone. God gave us one another to bear each other's burdens.

1 Corinthians 10:13
Galatians 6:13

MY AGING DAYS

My body's tired, I'm growing old,
And I need comfort for this soul.
But God has given me such peace,
That all this pain will someday cease.
So, bless the one who makes my bed
And shapes the pillows for my head.
Bless the ones who make me smile
And prays with me for just a while.
And bless the ones who hold my hand,
And let me know they understand
That now I'm old and very slow.
These days I'm waiting just to go.
So, thank you, for kind words that's said,
And God bless those who brought me bread.
Dear Lord, just love them; so will I.
We'll meet again, sweet bye and bye.

Cast me not off in the time of old age;
Forsake me not when my strength faileth.
Psalm 71:9

MY CHRISTMAS STORY

It was near Christmas time and everyone was decorating for the Holidays. The tinsel was rattling in the breeze and wreaths were hanging on the doors. The sound of Christmas music was in the air everywhere I roamed.

I decided I would go shopping. There was nothing I particularly needed but I always enjoyed shopping around in the mall during the Christmas Holidays.

I entered my favorite jewelry store and there it was, the same gorgeous diamond ring I had admired in the window a few days ago. The sales clerk said she would hold it for me until the next day so I walked out feeling very proud.

As I stepped around the corner, my eyes became fixed on a lovely lady in a wheel chair. She was pushing herself along by the wheels of the chair and looking up at a handsome man walking along by her side. There was a smile on their faces and a glow in their eyes as they chatted with each other. They appeared to be as happy as two kids anxious to visit Santa.

Suddenly, the gentleman reached over and assisted her in making a complete turn in the wheel chair. I stood in amazement when I saw this lovely lady had no legs, no legs at all, but appeared to have the joy of the Lord in her heart. I froze in my tracts and watched as they slowly disappeared from my sight. They showed so much adoration for each other. I stood there for a moment, reliving what I had just witnessed, and I knew they had something I wanted.

I hurried back to the jewelry store and asked the clerk if she could put the ring back out for sale. I explained how I had just witnessed true joy and happiness. The kind of joy I had just witnessed cannot be bought with a diamond, no matter how big or how beautiful.

When the joy of the Lord shines through one's face, it can magnify His Glory, and touch those around us. Much can be taken away from us but we can still have God's joy in our heart.

MERRY CHRISTMAS

MY COMPUTER AND I

Sometimes I think my computer was designed after my brain. Some days my computer works so slow I have to beg God for patience so I can deal with it. On the computer, I click a button to defragment the hard drive and boost its performance. In my brain I have fragmented files that need to be deleted or put in order so I can perform better.

When I'm working on the computer and nothing seems to go right, I cut it off for a few minutes and restart it. When the computer is cut off and restarted, it reprograms itself.

Sometimes my spiritual life needs to be restarted. I need to turn everything off and use a little quiet time to focus on God. Then patiently wait for his directions for removing obstacles that are causing problems in my life.

When my spiritual life is in order and my priorities are correctly filed, life runs much smoother.

MY GOD

Some say God, He is my master.
He's all the world to me.
Some say God is my redeemer
Who heals my every plea.
Some say God will ne'er forsake me,
He'll always bring me peace.
I will love my Lord forever,
His love will never cease.

Some say God can move the mountain
And calm the angry sea.
And my God, He can restrain me
And bring me to my knee.
But, some say God, I do not know him.
No, He is not for me.
Then one day when life is over,
My God will not know thee.

I say God, He is my shepherd,
Who leads me day by day.
And my God, He brings me comfort
Along life's weary way.
And when sin just overwhelms me,
He comes to set me free.
I say God, He is my Savior,
Who gives me life e-tern-i-ty.

MY MORNING TALK WITH GOD

Before I get off my bed this morning, I'm going to look back at my past and thank God for all my accomplishments and the many blessings I have been given. I will even thank Him for the bad times I have experienced through life because they have made me stronger. I will ask forgiveness for the things I have done that was not pleasing to Him. I will ask God to guide me through the day that I might do the right thing.

Then I will rise with a happy heart knowing that God will be with me through any difficulties I might face.

I will tell those I love just how much I love them and how important they are to me. If I don't tell them, they may never know. I will speak kindly to everyone I meet. I will tell a little child how special he is. When I go to the grocery store, I will help the elderly lady put her groceries in the car and return the cart to its rack. If I can find the courage to share God's love with one person, it will make my day.

As the night falls upon me, I will look to the heavens and stand in awe at the beauty of God's creation, the stars and the moon. When I lay my head on my pillow tonight, I will thank God for one of the best days of my life.

MY RAINBOW

Everyone gets excited when there's a rainbow in sight. We immediately point it out to whoever is standing nearby. We have an emotional connection with a beautiful rainbow. It calls our attention to God's creativity and beauty that he planned for our enjoyment. The magnificent colors energize us and lift our mood.

Rainbows can be seen whenever there are rain droplets in the air and sunlight shining from behind the observer at a low altitude angle.

Regardless of how the rainbow appears in the sky, I always connect it to God's promise that he will never again send a flood to destroy the earth.

Promises made by God are expressions of his love for us. He has never broken a promise. He is a God of love. He has always been faithful and truthful, and always will be. Letting his Son die on the cross for our sins was his ultimate expression of love. God is all powerful and all mighty. He is also in control and available for those who call on him.

God is like a rainbow in my life. He gives me joy and encouragement. He helps my faith grow stronger. The very thought of him lifts my mood and energizes my soul.

You can be a rainbow in someone else's life. You can bring joy, hope, and encouragement to someone who has lost their way. When you bring joy to someone else's life, you find more joy in your own life.

NEVER TOO LATE

Do you sometimes feel you have missed your boat? Do you have unused talents that are being wasted? Sometimes we can back up, reorganize and regain the opportunity to accomplish those deep desires of the heart. But more often, we have gone too far in life to turn back to the original desire for life. As we move forward, we make commitments that should not be broken. We have children to care for, financial obligations, and the list goes on. We always have other choices and, maybe, another direction for life would be best after all. Don't fret over things that cannot be changed. Move on to something that will fit in your life.

Make every day count and you will find that every day is a new day when you walk with the Lord.

OH, WHAT A SAVIOR

Sometimes we feel a need to talk with God about various things in life. After giving it some thought, we decide that our needs are such petty little things compared to those who have serious problems. We think, maybe God is too busy to be bothered by us. That's when we have to remind ourselves that God is right here just waiting and longing to hear from us.

In the still of the night, when sleep doesn't come as rapidly as we would like, we feel like the whole world is sleeping and here we lay with eyes wide open. The only noise is the cracking sound of the floor expanding or a slight whisper of the wind. But our God is not sleeping! He's patiently waiting to hear from us. What a perfect time to have a personal talk with our loving Savior

Ask the Lord for direction in your life. Ask Him to relieve you of your burdens. Ask Him to forgive you of your sins, whatever they may be. But don't forget to praise Him for His good works.

I pray that love, peace and joy find a permanent place in your heart now and forever. Amen

ONE DAY IN MY LIFE

When I awoke this morning and looked out the window, I found a winter wonderland right there in my back yard. It snowed during the night and was absolutely gorgeous so early in the morning before the squirrels and birds could make their tracks. I felt like God had cleaned the world and decorated it all at the same time. The snow was on the shrubbery and hanging on the tree branches. The chain linked fence in the back yard was coated making it look like a snow fence. No human hands could ever make something so beautiful.

I wanted so much to wake you and tell you about the snow but you were not there. I remembered other times while you were still with me, we would rush to the windows like two kids, so excited about the snow. A good snow always brought joy and excitement to our home.

South Eastern Virginia seldom has snow so I felt like God had to work overtime to bring such beauty to this earth.

I've always been told the first Christmas and first birthday after losing a love one is very hard on the ones left behind. The first snow was very hard too but I had fond memories just the same. Thank you, God. 1/28/2021

PLAN FOR A BETTER TOMORROW

Before you go to bed at night, think about what you will do when you rise in the morning. Never wake up in the morning thinking there is no reason for you to get off the bed. Start your day with prayer. Let your next thought be, "I know God has plans for me today."

God does have plans for you, but so often we fail to follow through with the plans God has for us.

Start your day early. It's easy to focus on God in the stillness of the morning. In the business of the day, it is hard to hear God when he offers you directions in life. Tell God how much you love him and believe you are going to have a good day. God will love you for it. He wants you to have peace and joy in your heart.

------he will be very gracious unto thee at the voice of thy cry; when he shall hear it, he will answer thee. Isaiah 30:19

PRAYER FOR OUR PEOPLE

Help us, Lord, to love our neighbor, even when they act in an unlovable way.

Give us courage to do your will, even when we would prefer to do it our way.

When things are beyond our control, give us courage to ask for your help and

your patience to wait for your guidance.

Help us to keep our faith in you, even during the toughest times of our life.

Help us to see your love in the beauty of each sunset, the twinkle of each star

and the fragrance of every rose.

Give us peace and joy in our heart so that we may know your joy, not just the

joy of the world.

Help us to be quick to listen, slow to speak and slow to become angry.

Let our hearts not be troubled, because you are in control.

Bless those who have been caught up in the senseless shootings in this world.

May those who have lost love ones find a means of forgiveness for the criminals and may they

find Your peace in their heart as they heal.

We pray for the safety of our country and our people. We pray for all the elected officials

in our government and those who are seeking election.

Continue-----------

Touch them, Lord, that they might make you a part of each political decision made.
We pray for a more peaceful world and pray that we have the courage to stand strong for
our faith in Christian beliefs. Let our Christian faith grow even while others are trying
to destroy our faith in You.

Forgive us for our sins and purify us from all unrighteousness. Let us be thankful
every day of our life for the sacrifice you made when you gave the life of your Son
and made it possible for us to enter the gates of
Heaven and live forever with you.
In Jesus name we pray. AMEN

PRAYER FOR THE NEW YEAR

Lord, as the old year ends and a new one begins, let us pause for a moment to thank you for all the blessings you have given us throughout the year. We know there have been times you had mercy on us and continued to love us in spite of the ugly things we have done, said or thought. We want to say, "thank you" for every gift you have given us and ask for your forgiveness of all our sins.

This being a new year, we find it a good time to start anew. We ask you, Lord, to give us the strength and courage to live a better life. Help us to be merciful, just as you are merciful to us. Even in the toughest of times, Lord, we pray that we can keep the faith to praise you. Make us quick to listen, slow to speak and slow to become angry. Give us patience we need to love our fellowman. Help us to be humble and give us the desire to stay focused on you and live a life that will be pleasing to you. Keep us close to you and shower us with your grace and mercy as we travel through life's amazing journey.

Amen

PRAYER OF GRATITUDE

Lord, I would like to take this time to say, "Thank You." Thank You, for always being there for me when I need you. Thank you, for the unconditional love you have for all your children.

I know that every good gift and every perfect gift comes from you. I pray that you find me grateful every day for all your gifts, spiritual and material.

Lord, I thank you for being close to the broken hearted and those who are crushed in spirit.

My God, you fill my heart with joy and peace even when I think there's no joy left to be found. You have a plan to fulfill my every need, and I thank You from the bottom of my heart.

Lord, I pray for the destruction of any evil group that is trying to destroy our Christian faith.

I pray that you will not be left out of the decisions made at the voting polls and may your presence be known among the leaders of this country.

I know without a doubt, there is but one God and you sacrificed the life of your Son so that your people could be forgiven of their sins and one day live with You in Heaven. Hear my prayer, O God. Amen

MY ROSE OF SHARON

Do you ever stop during your busy day and look around to see and enjoy the beauty of God's wonderful world? Maybe that's something we need to start doing more often, even if we only take five minutes out of our schedule. Concentrating on God for five minutes is a good place to start for one who is not in the habit of spending time with God.

Sometimes we look but don't really see, and therefore, fail to give God the Glory for His marvelous creation. Other times we listen but don't really hear and understand the message we should be getting.

I can see some beauty in most everything I look upon. I also see God's hand in the creation of all things; in the growth of a plant, the beauty of a flower, the setting of the sun, the angry rolling sea, or the roaring thunder clouds. But I always know and acknowledge the fact that God is in control.

Through the years we have been told many times that we should stay focused on God. And you might ask yourself, "How do I stay focused on God when there is so much going on in my life and so many distractions around me? When we are focused on God, we can see the world in a whole different light and God's creation can have a new meaning.

On the patio just outside my kitchen window, is a lovely Rose of Sharon bush.

Continue-----------

When it's in full bloom, I find myself standing by the sink, gazing out the window at the gorgeous blooms on that bush and maybe daydreaming. I understand there are several varieties of the Rose Of Sharon but I can only tell you about the one I have watched grow and bloom through the years.

One day while I was washing dishes and enjoying the blooms on my bush, I began to see it as a work of God, not just a lovely flower. The bush is pruned every spring to shape it and to keep it the size I want it to be. Pruning can cause new growth and the blooms for the summer will come on the new growth.

Pruning the bush reminds me of the times our pride prevents us from living the way Jesus would have us live. So God, sometimes, finds a way to cut us back a little so we can continue to grow in wisdom and in spirit.

That brings to mind an old expression moms used to use when a child got too smart mouth. She might say, "Alright big boy, you are getting too big for your britches." So when we get too big for our britches, God finds a way to cut us back.

Each branch of new growth on the bush will develop a cluster of flower buds that will bloom throughout the summer. The buds in the cluster never bloom all at one time. Each one waits patiently for its turn to show its beauty. That reminds me that there is a time for everything, and sometimes we need to be patient and let God act on things in His time and in His own way. Life is full of opportunities just waiting to happen, if we will only be patient and trust in God.

Late in the evening, the blooms look very tired, as if

they had a busy day and need a good night of rest. Early in the morning, I'm greeted with a whole new crop of blooms that look so fresh. That reminds me that every day is a new day in Christ. So, when you are focused on God, you can read so much into a simple flower.

Back in the time of Solomon, Sharon was one of the largest valley-plains in all of Palestine. It was a fertile plain and was known for its beautiful flowers, including the Rose of Sharon. Many have referred to Jesus as the Rose of Sharon.

But nowhere in the New Testament is Jesus actually referred to as such.

The rose is said to be the most perfect of all flowers. Since Jesus is totally perfect in His own nature, maybe God, the Father, would approve of us using the Rose of Sharon to symbolize His Son's perfect love for us even though it is not actually stated in the scripture.

I've enjoyed my Rose of Sharon bush and I know it's only a flower but I can look at it and see God's hand at work. It's just one more creation that can stimulate the spirit and give such joy and beauty to those who love the Lord.

Lord, we thank you for all the beauty on this earth.
We thank you for loving us and always being there to lift us up and bear our burdens when life gets tough.
Thank you for this opportunity to share what's in my heart.
I pray that my thoughts might touch someone's heart and bring them closer to You. Amen

SATAN IS VERY REAL

Satan was a beautiful and powerful fallen angel. He was once the highest of all angels in Heaven. He decided he wanted to rule the universe. When his pride got in his way, God cast him out of Heaven.

The Bible warns us about our pride.

Satan still likes to lead our people into a rebellion against God. When Jesus was on earth, he personally faced temptation from the devil. We must learn to recognize Satan's intrusions into our thoughts and our life. If we are not careful, he will undermine our confidence in God's unconditional love. Satan hates all that God loves and will do whatever he can to destroy God's love. He does not want us to identify with the Lord so he leads people into sin because he knows it hurts people and God.

It is important that we remember that God's love is available to everyone. We have his love today, tomorrow, and forever. We must train our mind to trust God.

"Submit yourselves therefore to God." James 4:7

Resist the devil and he will flee from you as stated in Matthew 16:23 "Get behind me Satan! You are a hindrance to me. For you are not setting your mind on the things of God but on the things of man."

Micah 6:8 "----what doth the Lord require of thee, but to do justly, and to love mercy, and to walk humbly with thou God?"

If we walk humbly with the Lord, there will be no place in our life for pride.

SHARE YOUR ROSES NOW

When one's eyes are closed and their hands are cold, they won't be able to smell your beautiful flowers or see the glitter of a raindrop in the early morn. After they have been laid to rest, they won't be able to hear the kind words people will say about them.

When one's burdens are heavy and a smile no longer glows upon their face, kind words, understanding and encouragement can be a blessing to their heart. Everyone needs to be loved.

There is a wealth of unexpressed love in this world and when death comes to a loved one, it will hurt to think you will never have the chance to express that unspoken love. If you don't say it today, you may never have the chance to say, "I'm sorry" or "I love you."

God never promised us life on this earth tomorrow, so use today to the best of your ability and according to God's will.

SHE'S UP THERE SOMEWHERE

Hey, Mom, it's me again.
I still love you, after all these years.
I know you are up there somewhere,
Just waiting for me to join you.

You were such a good Mom.
I didn't always know that,
But I know it now, Mom.
I didn't always listen when you
Told me how bad your back hurt.
But you kept working just the same.
I understand it now, Mom.
My back hurts just like yours.
But I still take care of my family
And teach my kids right from wrong.
I'm just like you, Mom.

I remember a lot of things you told me,
When you thought I wasn't listening.
And I've forgotten a lot of things too.
But, I still know how much you loved me.
You always forgave me for any wrong doings.
You always protected me
And directed me down the right path.
No one could have a better Mom than you.

I never told you how much I loved you.
Well, not as often as I should have.
But I hope I showed it in other ways.

Today, I looked up at the sky, Mom,

Continue-----------

And I saw big white fluffy clouds
Just floating around up there.
I stood there and watched them
While they slowly changed.
They were so beautiful, just like you.
I saw angels in those clouds
And God's Glory shining all around.
Then I watched those beautiful clouds
As they slowly disappeared.

As I walked away, I said to myself,
"How beautiful Heaven must be,
And I know my Mom is up there
somewhere."

SO YOU THINK THERE IS NO GOD

Are there any true atheists in the world?

If so, why are they so bothered by the issue of people believing in God? Why does it bother them so much when we display biblical recordings in public places? Is it because God is pressing the issue and they can't escape thinking about the possibility of a God? He keeps the proof of his existence squarely before us all the time.

The universe has not always existed but the greatest scientists in the world cannot explain the sudden explosion of light and matter.

Tell me, who did the math when the earth was perfectly placed just the right distance from the sun so we do not freeze? If the earth was placed too close to the sun, we would burn. The earth remains this perfect distance from the sun while it rotates around the sun at a speed of about 1100 miles per hour at the equator. It rotates on its axis, allowing the entire earth to be properly warmed and cooled every day.

And that beautiful moon, is the perfect size and distance from the earth for its gravitational pull, but we'll save that for another time. For now, can anyone tell me, there is no God?

SOME CHOICES ARE
MADE BY GOD

So far as we know, it was the people's vote that placed Donald Trump in our presidential office. Or, could it have been God's plan?

During the first few months of the Presidential Campaign, only a handful of people believed that Donald Trump could ever become President of the United States of America. People saw him as an entertainer or celebrity. But, God can change things. He can change people, He changes circumstances and he can change the world. It's important that we remember what God has done, He can still do. Being so negative never helps anyone.

I challenge you to open your Bible and read the story of David becoming King. I Samuel 16:7

God decided to choose a new King for Israel so He chose one of Jesse's sons. Jesse had seven handsome and very strong sons but God rejected them. Instead, He asked to see the youngest son who was just a young shepherd boy. When God looked at David, He saw a king and said, "He will be the next king of Israel." David was not the oldest or tallest and he wasn't the strongest but God doesn't look at one's appearance, He looks at the heart. So, it was God's choice to make David the king of Israel.

Another scripture we need to study at this critical time in our country is 2 Chronicle 7:14.

Lord, help us to remember that we should not judge people by appearance but by what is in the heart. I pray that our people will humble themselves, turn from their wicked ways, ask for God's forgiveness and I pray that He will heal our land. Amen

SUNSET

Someone described the sunset as, "God's beautiful signature at the end of the day." That's a wonderful way to describe the sunset. It is different every day. Just to sit at the close of the day and watch it form its colors and change moment by moment, can be a breathtaking experience. This is just one of a billion ways God has marked our universe. There are so many places we could see God's signature if only we would look. So often we look but don't really see what's before our eyes.

I never studied art in great depth, but when I took an interest in art and tried my hand at drawing and painting, it really opened my eyes. I could see God's creativity in nature like I never saw before. God created everything, but everything is different, even the billions of twigs on the trees.

So it is with God's people. We are all different and we are all here to serve the Lord. So, when you are having happy moments, praise God. During the difficult moments, seek God. Use your quiet moments to worship God. During the painful moments, trust God and every moment of the day, thank God.

SWING'N ON THE GATES OF HEAVEN

Lord, you've been so good to me.
You've filled my every need.
You've washed my heart with love
And took away my greed.
Through the many storms of life,
You wiped away my tears.
You touched my heart with gladness
And calmed me of my fears.
I've been a faithful servant,
I know I sometimes fail.
I ask you for forgiveness
And make my life go well.
But now that I've grown old,
My mind is not so clear.
My legs are weak; my hands shake;
I always need you near.
I want to see my Jesus,
No longer want to roam.
I'm swing'n on the gates of Heaven
Singing, "Jesus, take me home."

TAKE TIME TO SMELL THE ROSES

There are many moments that could bring joy to our lives, but we often let them pass and never give them a second thought. Savoring the small joys can be uplifting and give us nourishment and strength to tackle the unpleasant things we face.. Some of the joy-making moments can come from the most unexpected places.

In a quiet time, recall some little thing that once brought joy to your heart. It can bring joy again if you will let it. Don't waste time dwelling on things you should have done, or unpleasant things that happened in the past.

A simple comment that brought you joy in the past can bring you joy for years to come. Take the time to recall that blissful moment.

Take time to visit a sick friend or one who has been down in the dumps for whatever reason. You might bring a little joy to their life, and quite often you will leave feeling uplifted and glad you made a much needed visit.

Take a walk around the block or a walk in the park. Look for things that reveal the beauty of God's creation. Actually, stop and study the beauty of a rose or some other flower that might be in sight.

The more you rush through life, the more blissful moments you miss. Take time to smell the roses, even if it's just for a moment. You will be glad you did.

THANK GOD FOR PATIENCE

Many times I have walked down the hall asking God to give me the patience to handle a situation
or give me the words I might share with a person to give them peace and comfort. When my patience is not strong enough to handle the things that are coming at me, I have to call on my Lord. I need God's patience, His guidance and His love so I can love the unlovable moments I sometimes face.

Patience is the state of endurance under difficult circumstances. It is one of the most valuable virtues of life. It is part of the fruit of the Holy Spirit. Ecclesiastes teaches us that the end of a matter is better than its beginning and patience is better than pride. Thessalonian tells us that we should be patient with all. See that no one returns evil with evil; rather, always seek what is good for each other and for all. In Timothy, the Bible states that Jesus might display his unlimited patience as an example for those who would believe on him and receive eternal life.

But, sometimes the realms of glory seem too far away and, Lord, that's when I need you most.
Thank you, Lord, for patience!

THE AMAZING BUTTERFLY

There's something about the butterfly that captures my attention. Maybe it's their indescribable beauty or the magnificent color and design on their wings. Maybe it's the way they float through the air so gracefully, as if they want to show off their gentleness and beauty. Whatever it is, they get my attention and seem to soften the heart of all mankind. In my mind, I connect the butterfly with love, happiness, and freedom. It is evidence of nature's desire for beauty that can be shared with God's people.

There is an amazing life-cycle of these little guys who love to float around in my garden. They represent new life and transformation. Most of us like to watch the butterfly but seldom think about the changes it has to go through to achieve its beauty. Such beauty could never be invented by human genius.

Its life cycle begins when the female butterfly deposits a tiny egg upon a branch or leaf. Inside this egg grows a tiny worm-like grub which grows into a caterpillar with an enormous appetite. It eats a lot of leaves and stores food for its next stage of life. When it grows too big for its skin, it spins a case around itself and goes to sleep. At its given time, the case splits and a butterfly emerges. As soon as the wings are dry the butterfly is ready to find food, mostly nectar. The ugly worm has been transformed into something more beautiful than words can express.

Continue-----------

Like the butterfly, we can be transformed from a life of ugliness to a beautiful life of caring, loving, and forgiving. Sharp words can be replaced by responding with kind words. A frown can be replaced with a smile. A damaged relationship can often be repaired with an apology. Having a caring attitude toward others can brighten someone's day, as well as our own. But, in order to transform and complete our life cycle, we need to accept Jesus Christ, the Son of God, as our Savior. Then we can truly start to enjoy the wonderful love of our Heavenly Father.

THE AMAZING JOURNEY OF LIFE

Here we are beginning the last month of the year. My, how the time goes by! There are so many things I wish I could have done or would have done before the end of the year.

When we are young we look at life as if it has no end. We treat life as if we have forever to achieve the goals our heart desires. Too often we fail to use the abilities God gives us. Therefore, we leave this world without fulfilling our desires or God's desires for us.

Life is like a journey down a long winding road. We start out with a long list of beautiful plans, expecting each day to be even more perfect than the day before. But life is not always that simple. Life can start out like a joy ride but sooner or later we may reach a bend in the road and the most unexpected can happen.

It sometimes takes a bump in the road to wake us up to the realization that this Jesus we have heard about is very real. He is the Son of God. He was born of God and of a woman, without the help of a man. Jesus was in God's plan before He made man. He came to earth to die for our sins that we can have life everlasting.

Every one of us has the opportunity to talk with God and to know Him personally through His Son Jesus Christ. When we talk with God, it is not the muttered words we speak that concern Him, it is the attitude of the heart that gives Him joy.

THE CHRISTIAN FLAG

The Christian flag is one of the oldest unchanged flags in the world. It belongs to all but owned by none. The simplicity makes it easy to reproduce and there is no copyright associated with it.

The Christian flag was first conceived on September 26, 1897. Charles Overton, a superintendent of a Sunday school, was forced to give a lecture to some students when the scheduled speaker failed to show up. While giving the speech, Overton saw a flag of the United States displayed in front of the church. Drawing on the flag for inspiration, he gave the speech asking students what a flag representing Christianity would look like. After thinking about the lecture, Charles Overton and Ralph Diffendorfer designed and began promoting the Christian flag.

Since it was inspired by the flag of the United States, it takes its colors and overall design from the American flag. The cross is a symbol of pain and suffering of the crucifixion and spiritual sacrifice required of the followers of Jesus. The color red represents the blood of Jesus. Blood has been used since earliest Christianity to symbolize salvation through Jesus. The blue square represents faithfulness, truth and sincerity. The white background symbolizes purity and forgiveness as in the Bible, "though your sins be as scarlet, they shall be white as snow." Isaiah 1:18

THE NEW YEAR

Let's take a look at the New Year. We can look at it as a new beginning or we can look at it as just more of the same. Some people will go into the New Year expecting the worse while others will look at it with no expectation at all.

None of us know what the future holds, so I prefer to take what God hands me, and with God's help, make the most of it.

I pray that we will love the Lord with all our heart.

May we hope for the best but always be prepared if it is less.

If there is something we can do to make this world a better place, let us do it.

No matter what tomorrow brings, there will be a day that we cannot make it on our own, and we are going to need the Lord.

When the day comes that our burdens are too heavy to bear, I pray that God will give us His grace and His mercy to make it through the difficult time.

God bless you and have a
"HAPPY NEW YEAR."

THE POWER OF PRAYER

I have climbed many mountains and crossed many bridges in the past, but I think the most horrifying moment in my life was the day my doctor called and gave me the report on my breast biopsy. He said I had a very rare kind of cancer and he had checked around and found the best doctor to handle my case.

My granddaughter was with me at the time, and after the initial shock, she said,

"Grammy, I'll pray for you." We stood holding hands, and she prayed the most beautiful prayer I have ever heard.

The weekend before my upcoming surgery, a new pastor came to our church for the congregation to meet him. My husband told him my surgery was coming up, and he didn't hesitate for a moment but immediately said, "Let's pray for her right now." Needless to say, he won my vote.

Every way I turned, someone was saying, "I'm praying for you." Maybe they prayed or maybe they didn't, but it was encouraging and made my faith grow stronger.

On my fifth year check-up, my doctor walked in with a glow on his face and said, "It's been five years!"

Thank God, I am still cancer free. I will always be grateful for those who cared enough to pray. I have often wondered how some people go through the tough times of life without knowing the love of Jesus Christ.

THESE HANDS

As I look at my hands, I think about how blessed I have been and how these hands have served me, served others, and served the Lord through the years. They are rough and wrinkled with age now, but they have served me well.

The fingers are crooked but they still hold my wedding band. These hands are growing weak but have been the tools I have used throughout my life to reach out to grab and embrace life. They have prepared food for me, my family, and my friends. They have put food in my mouth and clothes on my back.

They held the hands of my best friend as she was leaving this world to be with the Lord. They stroked and caressed my first puppy to make him calm. They also stroked his head while he was dying as an old dog. He was the most loyal friend one could ever have. These hands held my little new born baby when he entered this world, and then my grandchildren.

These hands remind me of where I have been, the things I have done, and the things I shouldn't have done. One day God will reach down and take these hands and lead me home. I can just imagine using these hands to touch the face of God and feel His hands upon my face. Hopefully, I will hear him say, "Well done my good and faithful servant."

What have you done with your hands?

Just something to think about!!!

THINGS CHANGE

As time goes by, everything on this earth changes. Our needs, our wants and desires in everyday life changes. Things that were so important to us are no longer important. That mink coat we thought we couldn't live without some years ago is now hanging in the back of the closet taking up some much needed space. Our kids don't want it, and it cost so much we hate to get rid of it. Did we really need it when we bought it? Why do we get caught up in worldly goods?

This world is changing so much and so fast, we worry about our children's future. We worry about security and their education.

The way we dress when we go to church has changed. We thought we should wear our best clothes when we go to God's house to worship him. Even I have fallen into the trap of dressing very causal when I go to church, but out of respect for God, I will never dress to the extreme like some.

Communication has changed. Modern technology has taken over the world. The majority of the population, especially the young, wants every piece of new equipment that comes out. Technology changes so fast it is impossible for the seniors to keep up. We often feel we are just left behind to fall through the cracks.

Even the Bible has changed through the years. There are a number of different versions of the Bible, each one written a little different. Sometimes, I wonder why some of the scripture has been rewritten when the old one is written as clearly as the newer version.

Continue-----------

With all the variations of our Holy Bible, we are so thankful that the basic story of God, the Father and Creator, Jesus Christ, our Savior, and the Holy Spirit, has not and will not change. If for some unknown reason my Bible is ripped from me, the story will not change but will always be planted in my heart forever and ever. This is the one thing that will never change.

THINGS TO REMEMBER

Remember the kind words others have said to you that made you feel loved and respected. Remember those who have given you words of encouragement along life's way. We sometimes need those words to make it through an uncertain time of our life.

If you are holding hurtful things in your heart, just cast them out as if they never happened. Life may not be what we had planned, but sometimes we have to make the best of what we are given. Don't do or say anything today that you will regret tomorrow.

Remember it is not wealth and finery that makes a person happy. These are just temporary fixes to the problem. It's the little things, in its own special way, that lets you know you are loved. It's those little things in life that give you that 'feel good moment' you never forget but treasure forever. Maybe it's that little kiss on the cheek by your spouse or child early in the morning when they thought you were still sleeping. Those little things can melt your heart and start your day off right.

Remember that trustworthy friend that stood by your side, no matter what the circumstances. A trusted friend is greater than a treasured possession.

Remember the times you have called on the Lord and he helped put your world back together when you thought it was falling apart. Remember to stay close to Him. You may need to call on him again, so praise his name every day. He'll be there when you call on him.

TRUST

The groundwork for true friendship is trust.

We have to build this trust before we can pour out our hearts and share everything with another person. We can tell a trusted friend things we don't even want to tell ourselves. A true and trusted friend will listen and not judge us for the mistakes we have made in the past.

You can consider yourself blessed if you have one such friend in a lifetime because they are not easy to find. To talk with someone about those mind-boggling things that get heavier every day can give us much relief.

Isn't that the way it is with God? We have to learn to trust him before we can lay all our troubles at his feet and expect him to take care of them and lead us in the right direction.

As the old familiar song goes:

> "Trust and obey for there's no other way to
> be happy in Jesus, but to trust and obey."

TWENTY THIRD PSALM

The Lord is my shepherd;
**God is watching over me like a shepherd
watching over his sheep**
I shall not want.
**I will never want for anything because
God will supply all my needs.**
He maketh me to lie down in green pastures:
**He will let me rest and be free of fear,
tension and hunger.**
He leadeth me beside still waters.
**He will give me confidence to face the
trials of the day under his leadership.**
He restoreth my soul;
He will heal and restore my spiritual life.
He leadeth me in the paths of righteousness
for his name sake.
**He will lead and guide me through paths
that will lead me straight to Heaven.**
Yea, though I walk through the valley of
the shadow of death,
**I will be challenged to walk through valleys
of dark shadows.**
I will fear no evil: for thou art with me;
**I will not be afraid because I have the
assurance that my God is with me.**
Thy rod and thy staff they comfort me.
The shepherd's symbol of strength is his

Continue-----------

staff that he uses to guide his sheep. I find comfort in knowing the power of God.

Thou prepares a table before me in the presence of mine enemies.

God prepares the way for me and with God'S help I must destroy evil that stands in my way.

Thou anointest my head with oil; my cup runneth over:

No matter how I live my life I can expect some bruises and hurts but God is always there to comfort me and ease my pain.

Surely goodness and mercy shall follow me all the days of my life:

I won't fill my mind with negative thoughts but begin each day with hope.

And I will dwell in the house of the Lord forever.

God has promised me a home with him where I shall have eternal life.

{A Psalm of David with my interpretation}

UNANSWERED PRAYERS

Just because God doesn't answer a prayer doesn't mean he no longer cares or he has forgotten us. If we ask and don't receive, we may have asked for the wrong motive or for our own pleasure. If our wickedness has made a separation between us and God, he may not hear. We must ask in faith without any doubting. God does not answer prayer because of the pride of evil men. God will hide his face from those who are practicing evil deeds.

We will make all kinds of promises if only God will give us what we want. Other times, we think we know what's best and we tell God what we want instead of asking God to direct our lives his way.

God's greatest gift sometimes is when he says "NO".

We don't always know what's best for us. We can't see into the future but God can. Maybe he has something better in store for us.

When we think we are in total control of our life, we can easily lose faith in God because we are no longer dependent on him. Faith is what carries us through many tough times.

WAKE UP AMERICA

We are preparing to celebrate the birth of our Lord and Savior, Jesus Christ. While we are sharing the joys of Christmas, there are others who are preparing to destroy us and all Christians in the United States, in the Middle East and elsewhere.

I watched the television while Christians were standing in line waiting to be beheaded by a group called, "ISIS." It reminded me of the brutality Jesus suffered by the Roman soldiers when they were ordered to kill him. Jesus was killed because he claimed to be the Son of God. Will we be killed because of our Christian faith?

If we had to face ISIS today, how many of us would stand up for Jesus or would we deny we ever knew him?

Wake up America, our country is in great danger and we the people want to know if we are going to sink with the ship or stand and fight for Jesus?

"MERRY CHRISTMAS"

WHAT A DIFFERENCE
A DAY MAKES

What a difference a day makes! Twenty four little hours can change ones whole life. The loss of a love one can take away much more than a companion. After the loss of someone near and dear to us, we are constantly reminded of the void they have made in our life. The decisions we make today can have a long term effect on our life, whether it be good or bad.

Maybe we have prayed for a long time and never gave up because it is very important to us. Then one day God opens the door and our dream comes true, what a joy that would be after we have patiently waited so long. We need to trust God and do as we are told if we want results.

The joy in our heart can be wiped away very quickly for many different reasons. But, when we are careful to choose the right decisions, for the right reasons, we are likely to get good results.

Sometimes one can live their life without the Lord and not even realize it because they never really knew the Lord. God is always by your side even if you don't know him. Once you wake up and realize that God is real, he loves you, and he wants you to lean on him, that's when you will know, "what a difference a day makes."

WHAT HAVE WE DONE FOR JESUS

How many times have we had the perfect opportunity to introduce someone to Jesus and we failed to do so?

How many promises have we made but didn't keep?

Do we sometimes mislead people for our own benefit?

How many times have we told someone, "I'll pray for you," and never thought of it again?

Do we sometimes feel like there is a force behind us telling us to go, speak up, share your thoughts, but something holds us back? Is it because you don't know exactly what to say? Remember, Jesus said if I send you I will tell you what to say within the hour.

Do we thank God for the many pleasures in life that He provides for us?

Do we trust in God continually or do we only trust in Him when we need Him most?

Do we skimp on the undivided quiet time we spend with God?

Have we learned to lean on Jesus or do we rely on our own strength? Every time we affirm our trust in Jesus, we are putting treasures in Heaven. When we lean on Jesus and trust in Him, He delights in our trusting confidence.

Do we want to make things happen before their time? This can cause us much stress because our time is not always God's time.

Sometimes, we need to put the world on hold while we take time to focus on God. We can only have one Master, so seek to please Jesus above all else. If we walk through the days ahead with our focus on Jesus, we will find that we are on the best roadmap available.

WHEN GOD TAKES ME HOME

I don't understand or fully comprehend all that the Bible tells me. But, there are some parts that really grab my attention. For instance, creativity has always been of great interest to me. I find the story about God's creation of the Heavens and the earth, the fact that he formed man from the dust of the ground is exciting to learn. All the other things he created, that I see around me every day, bring a lot of joy to my heart.

I am not a history loving person, so all the Kings, the wars and etc. don't hold my attention as much as it should. But, I know they played a very important part of the Bible.

Another part of the Bible that amazes me is the birth of Jesus Christ and the fact that God sacrificed his Son for our sins that we might have everlasting life.

Then, there's Heaven. Heaven is a real place. Jesus referred to it as "my Father's house." Heaven is a city designed and built by God. (Hebrew 11:10). The Bible doesn't tell us all we would like to know about heaven, but, it tells us everything we need to know. The word of God has painted a marvelous picture in my mind of what heaven must be like.

Heaven is so indescribable, the scriptures tell us that no man has ever seen, heard or even imagined what wonderful things God has in store for those who love him. The glory

Continue-----------

of God illuminates it. It is the place where God, the risen Christ, the angels and the Saints reside. It is the future home of the redeemed. There will be no pain, no suffering, and no tears there.

When I die, this old worn out body will remain in the casket, deep in the grave, but my soul shall rise and go to Heaven. There I shall meet my Lord, face to face. All the imperfections of this life will be removed. I can hardly wait to see what the perfect me will look like.

There is hope for all and there's room for all!
SEE YOU THERE!!!!!!!!!!!!

WHY JESUS WAS BORN

The birth of Jesus is the most significant event in all history. Family and friends are more likely to come together at Christmas than any other time of the year. We shower each other with love and gifts and often find it to be the right time to forget and forgive some wrong doings.

Without Christ, we could never become the person God would have us be. Jesus had to be born because mankind would have been eternally lost after the sins of Adam and Eve. Jesus had to come to earth and allow himself to be sacrificed to save mankind from its sins.

Thousands of years after Adam and Eve failed to carry out God's mandate to glorify Him in their lives, it was left up to Jesus to fulfill the devine revelation of God's character that gives us the desire to become more like him in mind and spirit. The Jesus we know today was made possible on that great celebrated day we call Christmas.

WILL YOUR PET GO TO HEAVEN

Dogs make wonderful pets. They love regardless of what kind of mood you are in. They are always glad to greet you when you come home. They can cheer you up when you are sad. They are great companions. They will alert you if a stranger arrives. Most of them will protect their master if they are about to be harmed. Families can become greatly attached to their pets and grieve when they have to bare the loss of one. Couples, who are childless, relate to their pets as if they are their children. Some even want to know if their pets will meet them in heaven, while there are others who truly believe that pets do go to heaven.

The book of Isaiah, Chapter 11:6-9 suggest that there will be animals in Heaven living in peaceful coexistence. However, we cannot conclude from the scripture that our pets will or will not be in Heaven. I have never read anything saying they will be resurrected even though there is mention of animals existing in the future.

There is one thing I am very sure of. If you believe and trust in Jesus Christ, God will take you into Heaven to live with him. When you get to the pearly gate and meet Jesus face to face, that will be a glorious day. You'll have no more tears or sorrow. What I also know is, if you do not believe and trust in JESUS CHRIST, you will not be there and will never know if your beloved pet went to Heaven or not. So accept Jesus as your Savior today and get the full assurance that you will go to Heaven. If you find your beloved pet there, He will be so happy to greet you.

YOU ARE GOD'S MASTERPIECE

Your body is a complex creation made by the hands of God. Each little part of the body has its function and if a person is in average health condition, the heart is beating 60 to 70 times per minute. The brain is storing away information. Cells are being formed and cells are being destroyed. The liver is detoxifying the blood and the body's entire blood supply is washing through the lungs. These are just a few of the many things going on in your body and you are not even aware they are happening.

Your life was planned long before you were born. You were created by the most powerful hands in the universe. God understands your thoughts and he understands every motive behind those thoughts. He also understands the motive behind everything you say or do. God loves you no less than he loves the next person.

You see, God made someone very special when he made you. Will you take a moment to ask forgiveness for any negative thoughts you may have and give thanks for all the blessings God has showered upon you?

You are truly God's masterpiece and don't let anyone tell you otherwise.

PRAYERS

TALKING WITH GOD

ASKING FOR DIRECTION IN LIFE

PRAISING GOD

THANKING GOD

SHARING YOUR BURDENS WITH GOD

ABOUT PRAYING

You don't have to be a public speaker to pray. God makes each of us different and does not give us the same talents. You just need to know that Jesus is the best friend you will ever have. He is always there for you, to direct your life and fill your needs. All you have to do is ask for his help and guidance. You can talk with him any time or any place and he will hear you.

While my husband was ill, I cared for him and there were times I was not sure I could emotionally and physically fill his needs for the rest of his life. But, with the help of the Lord I was there for him until his last breath. Many times I have walked down the hall praying, "Lord, give me the strength and patience to handle whatever I must face today. I need your love and direction every hour of every day. And, I thank you, Lord."

Praying is sharing with God what is in your heart and asking for his help and guidance in your daily life.

Don't forget to thank him for what he has done for you and praise him for the wonderful Father that he is.

LEARNING TO PRAY

To pray does not mean you are always asking for something tangible. You could be asking Jesus to come into your heart or to stand by you in a difficult time. If you are praying in the presence of others, you don't have to impress them by praying a long prayer or use big words, just keep it simple. Sometimes, it is good to go to a room and close the door, shutting out all distractions and talk privately with your Lord. He already knows what you need before you ask but that doesn't mean you should not tell him your needs.

God wants you to lean on him and admit your inability to meet your own needs. You can pray just to give God praise and honor. Thank him for all the wonderful things he has done for you. Thank him for helping you through the bad times. Just know he will always be there for you. He will never leave or forsake you.

CHRISTMAS DINNER BLESSING

Lord, we thank you for this special day,
a day to always remember the birth of
our Lord and Savior, Jesus Christ.
Thank you for this food you have provided
and we ask that you bless it for the
nourishment of our bodies. Bless the hands
that have prepared it and may it give us
strength and courage to be more like you.
In Jesus name we pray. Amen

MY PRAYER

Lord, I pray that we will keep the
faith to praise you, even in the
toughest of times. When things
are out of our control, give us
patience to wait for your guidance.
Help us to be humble so we can focus
on you. As we travel through life's
amazing journey, Lord, keep us
close to you and shower us with
your grace and mercy.

Amen

....

"And whatsoever ye shall ask in my name,
that will I do, that the Father may be
glorified in the Son.
If ye shall ask any thing in my name, I will
do it. John 14:13, 14

NIGHTTIME PRAYER

Thank you, Lord, for the accomplishments I made today. Now as I lay my head on my pillow, may I rest peacefully while you watch over me and protect me until I rise in your wonderful world in the morning.

AMEN

....

MY TRAVELING PRAYER

I ask you, LORD, to take control
of these four wheels on which I roll.
Lead me safely down busy streets,
And make me kind to those I meet.
I thank you, Lord, for one more day
You give me life and lead the way.

PRAISE AND GLORY

Lord, we know this life is not all there is and we know the best is yet to come so help us to live our lives in a way that honors you. May we be worthy of your grace and mercy while on this earth. Help us to never forget to give you all the praise and glory you deserve. Help us to share your love with others that they might come to know you better.

We pray in Jesus name. AMEN

PRAYER FOR A SICK FRIEND

Lord, I don't know exactly what to say, but, I know you are the almighty. I know you love all your children and you know our every need. Thank you for being such an awesome Father.

Lord, I have a friend, (name), who has that awful disease of cancer. She needs to know that you are with her through this troubling time. I pray that you will give her peace of mind and comfort. I pray that she will learn to lean on you and put her trust in you. And, Lord, if it will be your will I pray that you will touch her with your healing hand and make her whole again.

Be with her family and friends, Lord, and give them peace of mind. I pray this in Jesus name. AMEN

PRAYER FOR OUR COUNTRY

God, we believe you can change people, you can change things, you can change circumstances and you can change the world. So, we put all the evil doings in your hands and ask you to fight the battle for your people in this country. With your leadership and our willingness to change and be changed, the world can be a better place.

We pray for the safety of our people and safety of our troops and all security personnel. Bless all those who serve our country for the protection of our freedom.

Lord, help us that we might pray more often and worry less. Help us to know you hear our prayers and help us to wait patiently for your response. In Jesus name we pray. AMEN

PRAYERS FOR CHILDREN

Thank you, God, for loving me and I thank you for my Mom and Dad.

Amen

....

Thank you, Jesus, for a fun day. Watch over me while I sleep through the night.

Amen

....

Jesus, I love you. Help me to be a good boy   (or girl) tomorrow so I can have my Birthday Party.

Amen

....

Thank you, Jesus, for watching over me and keeping me safe. Thank you for my friends and family.

Amen

....

Thank you, Jesus, for this good food Mom cooked tonight.

Amen

THANKSGIVING BLESSING

Thank you, Lord, for all the wonderful
blessings you shower upon us.
We thank you that we have food on our
table while there are others who have
none. Lord, please, give them your
blessings.
Thank You for friends and family who
are here to share this food that You
provided. Bless the hands that
prepared it for this wonderful
occasion. We ask now that you use
this food for the nourishment of
our bodies. Make us strong and healthy
and worthy of your love.

In Jesus name we pray. Amen

Printed in the United States
by Baker & Taylor Publisher Services